CONFIDENCE
and *strength*

I HOPE YOU GAIN STRENGTH FROM THIS BOOK. BE BLESSED!

CONFIDENCE
and *strength*

Genelle Aldred

Fresh Inspirations

First published in England by Fresh Aspirations Ltd, February 2015

ISBN: 978-0-9931952-0-4

Printed and bound by Book Printing UK
Peterborough, Cambridgeshire

This book is dedicated to
my nieces, Krystal and Arooj.
As you grow up may you keep the
confidence and strength you already have,
which I admire so much.
X

Foreword

Being confident and strong is about knowing who you are and becoming the best version of you that you can be. Your uniqueness invites opportunity (as you are the only one who can do what you do). You become better at occupying the space in this life that is the perfect fit for you.

I am of Jamaican heritage, and there's a saying the Jamaicans use that I love! "Wi lickle, but we tallowah," in English: "we are small but strong". This inspired me to put a tallowah book together, something short, but powerful enough to anyone who reads it a boost of confidence and strength.

This book is a combination of lessons I've learned, tips I've heard, blogs and Facebook posts I've written AND quotes that have inspired me. I can't claim to have all the answers, but I hope that something in this book inspires you.

Genelle

What you do today can impact all your tomorrows

-Ralph Marston

Contents

Definitions

CONFIDENCE

1 The feeling or belief that one can have faith in or rely on someone or something

1.1 The state of feeling certain about the truth of something

1.2 A feeling of self-assurance arising from an appreciation of one's own abilities or qualities

STRENGTH

2 The capacity of an object or substance to withstand great force or pressure:

2.1 The emotional or mental qualities necessary in dealing with difficult or distressing situations

You Can Be Confident

Whether you feel confident or not is, in my opinion, largely based on what you believe. Let's be honest, we have all looked at someone else and thought, "HOW are they so confident? They are deluded!" Because when we look at their situation, status and – in all honesty – looks, sometimes we wonder how they can manage to feel the way they do, in spite of those things, particularly when we feel like a train wreck most of the time! It is what they *believe* to be true that gives them their confidence. But what is a belief?

1 An acceptance that something exists or is true, especially something without proof

2 Something that one accepts to be true, or real

What do you believe about yourself?

And, does what you believe about yourself make you feel confident about who and what you are, or not?

Something doesn't have to be true for you to believe it. For a long time in my early 20s I believed that I was really ugly. I used to cry about it and blamed my terrible looks for every problem I felt I had. "Nonsense!" Said friends and family, who love me very much, but until I believed I was actually alright looking, my false belief dictated how I felt. At that point, my confidence was at an all-time low.

That belief was a limiting one, and a major part of building your confidence will be confronting your own limiting beliefs. Whatever they are, however long you have had them, and whoever planted the idea, in order for your confidence to grow you must believe positive things about yourself, things that are uplifting, inspiring and true.

Being confident doesn't mean that every day you will be walking on sunshine or that you'll never have doubts and all fear is banished forever. We are all human and so we will, unfortunately, have bad days. This is when, to me, confidence is like courage. Sometimes you will doubt your decisions, your abilities, the way you look, the way you dress; confidence is to those things what courage is to fear: the ability to push through and continue. Confidence means that whenever issues and situations crop up, you know and believe and these positive, uplifting and inspiring truths.

**You can be confident in who and what you are.
You have what it takes. You can get back up.
You're not going to give up. You can do this!**

If you begin to believe in these affirmations, they will help to carry you through many situations. It's about having a confident belief system hard wired into your brain.

"I've learned that courage was not the absence of fear but the triumph over it"
— Nelson Mandela

It's Not All About Where You Are Now

Diamonds
used to be
coal

Life is a process. We are all works *in* progress. Don't be too hard on yourself (or anyone else). Just keep working at being better, knowing that it takes time.

Become Strong Enough To Be The You, YOU Want To Be

One persons too much (or not enough) is someone else's perfection.

As children we are just ourselves, we don't know any other way to be. We speak our truth, we say no, we are mainly selfish and we just do what we want to do. As we grow up all those things are chipped away. Some of those attitudes do need to go. The human race would probably not do so well if we all said what we felt whenever we wanted to. But it can go too far the other way. Which ends up with many of us too scared to be who we want to be. We choose a life of rolling over and playing dead over being assertive enough to say 'actually that is not for me'. We continually pretend to be someone else other than who we really are. We get 'rewarded' for being this other robot, we lose the confidence to do and say what we want, even when we *need* to. Mainly because we are fearful of feeling hurt if we are not accepted for who we really are.

If you were truly you, living your truth, being who you wanted to be in a way that respects others, what is the worst that can happen?

I have tried this out myself and found that the people who don't really like you anyway may not stick around. However, the ones who are truly for you will continue to embrace you, and these are the people you need around you. Our human instinct is to pursue relationships and companionship; even the most confident person wants to be liked. But it is better to be surrounded by the few who will build you up than the many smiling assassins, who are just waiting for you to trip and fall.

Be confident in who you are. Defend your right to be yourself as you would for a best friend. You are important and valuable and you have something to offer this world. Someone is counting on you to be you, so they can be themselves, too.

I am always very honest with myself about my good and bad points. I don't want to be deluded, thinking of myself as some kind of angel. I have my moments, and that's OK, because no one is perfect. I certainly cannot claim to be. What I believe about my core is what really counts. I am love, light and inspiration. That is who I am. So, if I am mean, or do something unpleasant, I know that I can apologise and move on, because the core of who I am is better than that. That's how I became confident about who I am. I got to know what, at my core, the best of me is.

There is only one you in the whole world. No one has the same mix of personality, attributes, skills, gifts and talents as you do. You are truly a one off. Own it! Don't waste your life chasing another's uniqueness when you already have your own.

"Develop enough courage so you can stand up for yourself and then stand up for somebody else"

— Maya Angelou

Every Day Is a New Chance

EVERY morning when you wake up you get a *fresh chance* to be BETTER than you were yesterday

USE IT!

I like to think that each day is a fresh start, with no mistakes in it. If you woke up this morning, then there is more life to be lived.

It's The Fight of Your Life

The biggest fight that you will continually have (and that you CAN continually win) is with yourself. Once you figure out how to face down the enemy within, you will grow in confidence and strength

The thing that almost stopped me from doing so many things was the fear of what the faceless and voiceless 'they' would say.

I have come to the conclusion that some of the worst things we think people will say about us are some of the worst things we think about ourselves

I say this because unless someone has actually said these things to you, where do these words come from?

There are so many reasons why we have the thought patterns we do; our culture, family, background and life experiences all add to our thinking and beliefs. This can make our mind a battlefield when we are trying to make changes.

If we are not careful we can end up in no man's land. We cannot go back to who we were, but we cannot become who we want to be.

If we become stuck in that spot we will eventually become weak, not trust our instincts and fail to see our potential. We will be afraid to move forward but scared to go back.

The inner enemy must be disproved every time it tries to introduce thoughts that might hold you back. Limiting beliefs must be replaced with life affirming thoughts and actions.

The next time you want to move forward but feel like you can't. Listen to your thoughts. Get to know what pushes your buttons and most importantly what builds you up and strengthens you.

"We are afraid of the enormity of the possible"

-Emile M Cioran

Face Your Fears

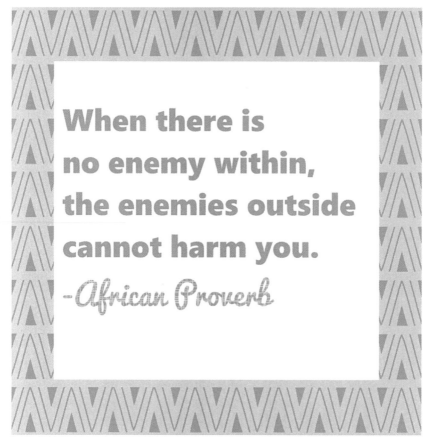

When there is
no enemy within,
the enemies outside
cannot harm you.

-African Proverb

A house divided against itself cannot stand. If there is a doubtful or fearful part of you holding you back from what you want, deal with it, so you can stay strong and move ahead with confidence

How Good Can You Stand It?

I first heard this question when listening to 'The Missing Secret' and it really made me stop and think.

How GOOD can you stand it?

Have you ever been presented with a 'no-brainer' opportunity, which you dithered about, and then didn't take because it seemed too good to be true? Something where you weren't able to trust that it was as good as it seemed?

Sometimes we are self-saboteurs because <u>we can't take it</u> when things are really good.

How many times have you heard "you can have too much of a good thing". Quite a few times, I imagine; it's almost pre-wired into us to not want too many good things to happen to us.

Look deep within yourself; what is the reason why you cannot accept that really good things can happen to you? Do you feel un-deserving? Guilty? Do you have low self-esteem? Want to be incognito? Feel like things will get bad again?

Think about that for a few moments, and just be honest with yourself...

We think if we have lots of money our family and friends will want it all, whilst disliking us for having it, that we won't be able to see who likes us for who we are, not what we have... And on and on we go.

Don't excuse yourself for being mediocre when greatness calls.

Scared that if we go for that promotion at work our colleagues won't like us anymore, that we won't have any 'friends', that people will think we're rising above our station... And on and we go.

We find our perfect partner and end up racked with insecurity; they are too good for us, they'll leave, they'll see us for who we really are, and so we're better off ending it before they do... And on and on we go.

At some point you must want to stop the vicious circle of self-fulfilling negative prophecies. Only you/me/we can do that.

My friend Lee said to me the other day: "The fear of success and failure are the same thing." I agree; they have different motivators but the same result: a crippling fear that stops you from being all you were meant and designed to be.

Fear is simply *False Evidence Appearing Real*

We must see ourselves as deserving, out there, bold and strong; it's more than OK to be all of those things. Shaking off other people's small-mindedness, negative thoughts and ill wishes and understanding that not everyone can stand it being good. If they can't stand it being good for themselves, you cannot possibly expect them to stand it being good for you!

So get over them, and get over yourself – yes, get over yourself. Get over the martyr inside that enjoys the pain of hopes deferred, because that's easier than the fear of having it good and then it all going bad. There will be highs and lows in life, that's a guarantee. But let the good be REALLY GOOD!

So ask yourself, "How good can I stand it?" If you realise that actually you may be the very thing that's holding you back from your dreams, then I have a suggestion... not advice, just a suggestion.

GRATITUDE! Become so grateful for everything that you have that you are consumed by it. The negativity of what you don't have will begin to disappear. Actually, feeling so happy for what you have helps you to understand how good you can stand it. Be grateful for your life, for waking up this morning, for those who love or have loved you, for those whom you love. If you have a job, be grateful; if you don't, then you have even more time to think of all the things you can be grateful for. Gratitude is a great place to start.

In order to be great, as great as we secretly dream of being, and to have the life we really want, we must be able to stand it being REALLY GOOD!

So let's get rid of the things that are holding us back, even if they are things within us. In fact, especially if they are things within us.

Bring your secret dreams and desires to the surface, and act on them. I don't want people to talk about my potential, I want to realise it, in full. When you can stand it really good you will find that all of the things you want will actually be drawn to you, because you will be ready for them.

When the question comes around again, "How good can you stand it?" I hope you/me/we can all honestly say: "REALLY GOOD!"

"You become what you believe"

– Oprah Winfrey

Get To The Other Side

EVERYTHING
YOU'VE EVER WANTED
IS ON THE
OTHER SIDE
OF FEAR.

- GEORGE ADAIR

This quote helps me to remember that the main reason I don't pursue most of the things I want is because I'm scared. But courage and a belief that you can face down that fear means you can go and get the 'thing' that you want!

The Perfect Plan

I believe there is a perfect plan for everyone's life. I believe in destiny and purpose. I also believe the reason why so many people go through life feeling hurt and discouraged is because we get things a bit muddled.

The fact that there is a perfect plan for your life does not mean your life will be perfect.

Maybe that loss, or the end of something, although it does not feel good right now, was the perfect way of getting you to where you needed to be for something else to come into your life, or begin.

I am learning to go along with the ebb and flow of life. Sometimes my plan, or the way I would like to control things or see them happen, is not THE plan. Often when we try to control things they still do not go the way we want.

Maybe it is time to try something new. The decision to let go and see the bigger picture can be daunting. But I just try to do my best, every time, allowing my steps to be ordered by more than just me, and it is paying off. I can be at peace knowing that I do not have to try and make things happen.

Next time your plans do not go the way you hoped, relax, open your heart, and ask yourself: "what's the lesson here, and what's the bigger plan?"

When Pope Benedict XVI came to England I was watching him on TV and he said something that I found so profound:

"Ask God what he requires of you, then ask him for the willingness to say yes."

Once you get into the flow of your perfect plan it will all become much easier; it will not be perfect every day, but when problems arise you will not get drawn into every single drama. Why? Because you will be able to see that it is all part of the bigger, perfect plan.

Ask for the willingness to say yes to your perfect plan.

The best time to plant a tree was 20 years ago. The second best time is today

—Chinese Proverb

You Are Right On Time

**Your journey has moulded you
for your greater good,
and it was exactly what it needed to be.
Don't think you've lost time.
There is no short-cutting to life.
It took each and every situation
you have encountered
to bring you to the now.
And now is**

right on time.

- Asha Tyson

This is your moment. Don't live in yesterday and don't wish today away so that tomorrow will come. Now is the perfect moment, enjoy it.

Seasons, Patterns and Cycles

Our lives are filled with seasons, patterns and cycles.

Just like summer, autumn, winter and spring. Just like a weather pattern of low pressure bringing rain and unstable weather, or a cycle of planting, watering, growth and harvest. My old pastor, Bishop Dave Carr, used to say to me, "look at nature and you'll learn about life".

Last night a conversation caused me to think about my seasons, patterns and cycles.

I realised that one of the hardest cycles to break is where a situation presents itself that FEELS like something you experienced in a previous season of your life, something that wounded you. You will often respond in the same way to the new situation as you did to the old one.

It is not that the situation is the same, the faces may have changed, and it could be a totally different scenario, but the way it makes you feel presents your mind with a dilemma. Precisely because everything has changed, apart from the way it makes you *feel*. It causes you to look back and wonder whether you have moved on at all.

When you have been very hurt by something, although it heals, sometimes the scar remains. The very presence of the scar is like a reminder of everything you never want to feel again.

Scars remind us that we too must heal

So if you are in a new season of life and trying to get into new ways of doing things, but the same old feelings rise up, this is a chance to change your pattern and break old cycles. Most of us, myself included, find it hard when we realise that we must try something new instead of reverting to what we have always known.

The feeling could be loss, rejection, loneliness or depression, and when you feel it coming it does not feel pleasant. It reminds you of those very situations you have spent time creating distance from, getting over and building yourself back up from.

After a trauma we utilise a series of coping mechanisms, which we put into place to help us, but more often they end up being our downfall, becoming almost like laws by which we must abide. The walls we build end up locking us in, and it can reach a point where we cannot find our way out. When this feeling starts to arise, everything within us moves instinctively towards our coping strategies, the same old patterns and cycles we are trying to get away from.

We pretend we are preventing ourselves from feeling any hurt, pain or sadness in life, and that is just not possible. In fact, these attempts have the opposite effect, because as well as experiencing these feelings anyway, we also become isolated.

If I feel a sudden loss or change coming on, my friends and family can tell you that I used to cope by cutting off. If I felt anything approaching something I did not like, I would cut you off, I would cut you out, I would shut you down and I would remove the person or the thing provoking my distress. The phrase 'throwing the baby out with the bath water' comes to mind. I would cut and run and most of the time never look back. More often than not, this didn't stop the hurt. It was time for me to find a way through instead of a way out.

Life is beautiful! Life is filled with so many blessings, but we have to accept that there is a side to life that does not always feel good. We have to realise that this is actually OK, and we will be OK.

We must let our scars be reminders that we can heal, not just reminders that we were once hurt.

It is a hard cycle to break, but if we have healed before we can heal again. If we overcame things in the past, we can overcome them again. If we managed to rebuild ourselves once, it can be done again. We can begin to break down the walls that have kept us in and everyone else out when we accept that any hurt, pain or loss can be gotten over, in time.

We do not need to fear the feelings that we felt before. We just need to know they may come again, and when they do, we can handle this and begin a new pattern, a new cycle. One that opens us up to being healed, being helped by others, not closed and isolated.

You might not achieve it every time. I might not achieve it every time. But if we want to move forward, we must try.

"It is never too late to become what you might have been"

-George Eliot

Embrace Your Season

I took this picture in North London in January 2013. It was winter and yet this Cherry Tree blossomed, whilst other trees were bare. Seasons change! Enjoy the summer season of your life. This tree cannot apologise and say, "Sorry that I'm flowering whilst you are bare." It just is. Enjoy your good seasons, and just be.

Antibiotics Don't Work on the First Day

Sometimes things get worse before they get better. That's just the way it goes.

Unfortunately, 'worse' often comes just as you are trying to sort a situation out. It can seem like a bit of a cruel joke.

It's like when you start clearing out old junk; as you start to take it out, it begins to look like it will never be clear. But, if you persevere you eventually clear it.

My mom is a very wise woman and she said to me:

"Antibiotics never work on the first day, and sometimes not even on the second. You want them to, but it takes time."

So my encouragement to anyone who is trying to sort themselves out, be that financially, career-wise or a relationship with a family member, friend or lover, keep going.

Sometimes it will get rocky, probably just as you start to apply the remedy, just as you start to do the 'right thing'. Take heart, stick with it, things will get better.

"Times will change for the better when you change"

-Maxwell Maltz

Never Stop

You are going to want to quit. *Don't!*

How many times do I want to give up? There have been so many times where I have almost given up! I've been down, but never out. You're not out either, so don't quit! Remember why you started and imagine how good you will feel when you're finished.

How Do You Judge Yourself?

We all sit in the judgement seat... I'd like to think I'm non-judgmental and unbiased, but I'll admit here and now that that's not always true.

The things we do not like in other people are the things we do not like about ourselves.

Now before you start huffing and puffing inside, "that's absolute rubbish". "I can't stand so and so and I would NEVER do what they do." Just take a few deep breaths and really think about it.

The only thing we want to see when we look in a mirror is a beautiful reflection. We don't want to see a spot, or a blemish, or a scar. But in every person there is imperfection. Sometimes the selfishness, meanness, manipulation we see in other people is what we really see reflected at us and this can be hard to accept. The other day I was called a spoilt brat by someone who I think is possibly the most spoilt, brat-like person I know, and they obviously feel the same way about me. Are either of us wrong? Probably not; it is all relative.

Let us all accept that we are imperfect.

BUT, a big, massive BUT, this is not solely what we should be judging ourselves on. It is very easy to beat yourself up, sometimes too easy. The other day I saw a powerful quote:

"Nobody has the right to make you feel worthless. Not even you."

–Unknown

The seat of judgment is a harsh place to sit in. It very often makes you feel bad about others, as well as yourself. We all fall short, and at times the reason we end up feeling so bad about ourselves is because the measuring stick we want others to live up to is one that we know we don't reach ourselves.

I'm a firm believer that instead of thinking about all the things that you have got wrong, try thinking about all the things you did right! Think about the things you have achieved, think about the things you are proud of, all of your many accomplishments! Judge yourself on those first. Then try to judge others in that same light.

Negative things are easier to remember than good things, bad memories and hurtful words linger longer. These negative words and memories are NOT who you are. Dig deep, remember the best of you. Surround yourself with people who love you, treat you well and lift you up. Think about how far you have come, what you have achieved, the good you have done in, and for, the world, think about your family and friends. Think well of yourself! There is brilliance in others and there is brilliance in you.

"Judge yourself by your BEST moments"

– Bishop Dr Joe Aldred

Who Are You Really?

*Close your eyes and imagine
the best version of you possible.
That's who you really are,
let go of any part of you
that doesn't believe it.
- C. Assaad*

Sometimes the person sabotaging all the good things you dream of is you; because you don't feel deserving, you think you're not good enough. Begin to believe that you are the best version of you. Talk like it, walk like it – you are it.

Flying Feels Good

You can't be afraid to make big and bold decisions.

You have to know yourself and what is it you really want from your life, because that's the only life you will live, your own.

I'm not against advice and opinions, but when the rubber hits the road, it's you who has to deal with the outcome, be it good or bad. Always remember you have to look yourself in the eye in the mirror every day, so use your conscience as a guide.

Here's what I do: I say a prayer, make the decision, close my eyes and take a leap of faith.

Flying feels good! :)

"She took a leap of faith and grew her wings on the way down"

-David Brinkley

Begin

IF WE WAIT FOR THE MOMENT WHEN EVERYTHING, ABSOLUTELY EVERYTHING IS READY. WE SHALL NEVER BEGIN.
-IVAN TURGENEV

Perfect moments are made when you begin. You can wait to be thinner, happier or richer. You might think you need to be more, or maybe less. You need to stop with the excuses and begin!

Light a Match

I once walked past a quote that summed up something I think many of us struggle with.

The hardest thing in life to learn is which bridge to cross and which to burn.

– David Russell

Can you relate to this? The feeling of, "How much more do I give, invest, do before I 'give up?' Should I give up? Is it even giving up, or is it wise to end this?"

I find these questions the most relevant to relationships; they are tricky things and you can find yourself giving and giving, being burned and hurt and still giving hoping that someone, or a situation will change. At times you can be treated badly or unfairly, and accept it. I've realised that I often do this out of fear that there is nothing better out there than what I currently have, even though it takes from me, burns and hurts me.

But I always remember what one of my gorgeous friends said to me about a situation she found herself in:

I looked at this guy and thought, is this my BEST LAST chance?

I still laugh about that to this day. Identify your bridge; it may be a lover, a friend, a job or something else.

To see your bridges go up in smoke is not great, and sometimes it's hard, but here are a few reasons why sometimes you have to burn a bridge. Make these points applicable to your situation.

1. You fell in love with someone, or something's potential – been there, done that! Are they fulfilling it? Can they?

2. You fell in love with a mirage – the guy/girl you fell in love in with isn't actually the person you are with; it's their representative, who was sent ahead to sell you a lemon, reel you in – and it worked.

3. You are the only one who walks across the bridge – if you constantly give and never receive, you will be drained and become a shell of the person you used to be.

4. You are no longer yourself – when your motivation and energy is sapped, your mojo has gone and your get up and go has left the room, it's time to reconsider who you are and what you actually want.

5. You think you can do better – YOU CAN!

The bridges to cross are the ones where, although the journey is tough, you feel energised and rejuvenated when you reach the other side. It's your passion. It's loving and being loved. Validation and encouragement.

You're not a bad person for walking away from something that you feel harms you. Like my mom always says:

I'm not anti-you, I'm pro-me.

It's hard to burn a bridge knowing that once you do there is no going back. At times you have to take the temporary pain to reach sustained success and happiness. This is scary, but necessary to get from where you are to where you want to be.

Ask yourself: "Is this my best last chance?" If it is, or even if the chances are very good and you have been 100% honest with yourself, it's a journey worth taking – GO FOR IT!

If it's not, light that match, let it burn.

"Fools take a knife and stab people in the back. The wise take the knife, cut the cord and free themselves from the fools"

– Unknown

Who Is Around You?

Surround yourself with the dreamers

AND the doers,

the believers and thinkers,

but most of all, surround yourself

with those who see the greatness within you,

even when you don't see it yourself.

— Edmund Lee

If the five people closest to you don't believe in you, you'll probably become the sixth unbeliever. Make sure there are people in your circle that can help to build you up, and take a moment to think about whether you really need the folk that tear you down.

Sade and Me

NB: This is blog I wrote on May 6th 2012. I have left it exactly as I posted it, mistakes and all.

On May 19th it will be 10 years since my pregnancy ended at 40 weeks and 10 days. My daughter, Sade was stillborn and I was just 19-years-old. She didn't open her eyes and she didn't cry. In fact I knew she wouldn't because after seven days of slow labour, and, seeing seven midwives from a rubbish hospital that I will not name, the contractions began coming fast. The student midwife could only hear my heartbeat when I arrived at the hospital with my mom, dad and sister.

So after several attempts to see if 'baby' was OK the registrar scanned me and said "There's no heartbeat."

I'd never even heard of a stillbirth at that time, only miscarriages. But when she said those words I knew exactly what she meant. My beautiful sister Alethea who had just left the room to call everyone and tell them I was in labour came back in and then had to go out and tell everyone the news. To this day I don't know how she did it. Just 18 at that time, then and now she's always been a rock for me. What followed was around 12 hours of emotional torture. I was bed-confined and epiduraled up. My mom, dad, sisters and bro-in-law came. My mom's best friend came, the paternal grandma and her sister came. And we all just waited for the baby to be born.

When you have a stillbirth you have to give birth naturally and that's one of the hardest things I've had to do. All the pushing and the crying, just no live birth at the end. Unless you've been through that you have no idea how it feels, believe me you can't imagine it either. So the baby was born and the sadness filled the room.

I'm not writing this to depress or scare anyone. But, I know there are thousands of women who have been through this who have never spoken about it.

Or they feel they can't speak about it. Women are pregnant all the time and we don't want to upset them. That's right too in a sense, pregnancy is difficult enough, but not enough women are aware that this does happen and awareness needs to be raised so it can be avoided. I also want to give women who have lost children a chance to say it happened to me, it affected me, and sometimes many, many years after the event it still hurts. Just because a child didn't take a breath on the outside of your belly doesn't mean they didn't exist.

So almost 10 years on and it feels like time to look back. I don't want to live in the past but it has shaped me. I want to share what I've seen and learned.

I've learned that LIFE GOES ON. It doesn't matter what you face, what you go through, how hard, tough, rough, bad and ugly life goes on. Since losing my daughter I've moved around ALOT, travelled, I've studied eventually getting my Masters in Broadcast Journalism, I've been a TV and radio presenter, a Weathergirl, a Virgin Atlantic check-in lady, A wedding gift list personal consultant. I've become an aunty, quite a few times. Seen nearly every single friend either get married or have babies or both. Sometimes it's tempting to sit down and want the world to stop. But if I did I would have missed out on all the wonderful things I've done and beautiful things I've seen.

I've learned that ANGER AND UNFORGIVENESS ARE CRIPPLING. I was very angry for a long time, with God, the hospital, life and anybody else who happened to get in the way. When you have a lot of anger inside it's like you're two people and the angry person is like a friend that you can't stand that you bump into all the time. You never know when they're going to show up. Unforgiveness does more harm to you than the person you're mad at. You have to carry them in your heart and remember what they did all the time. I bet the other person doesn't even remember what they did. These aren't helpful emotions, they drain you. They are heavy burdens and more and more things just get added all the time. In the end I couldn't keep up! I had to let all of that go. Let it go, for yourself.

I've learned that WORDS CAN BE WEAPONS. When I was pregnant my baby's father said some cruel things to me and they stayed with me for many years. I used to cry all the time and bless Holly! My gorgeous friend Holly she did moan but she listened and eventually I came round the realisation that what he said wasn't true. The words that leave your mouth can never go back. Think about it...

I've learned that PEOPLE CAN BE SO CRUEL AND SO KIND. From those who thought I should get over losing my baby three months after it happened to my family and friends. My parents have shown me so much love and understanding its unreal. My sisters who still send me mothers day cards and continue through the changes in their lives being so strong for me. My friends Audrey and Stephanie C who would knock someone out for me, who stick up for me and still let me talk about it when I want. They all do. My Jenny who made me countless cup of teas and prayed for me and listened. I LOVE my nieces and nephews. It was very hard at first to even look at pregnant people, never mind babies. Over time that has gone, but it did make me think more about sensitivities around those who have lost children and those who cannot have them at all. Although life does goes on can we be more caring and kind towards them instead of just wishing they'd get over it. They can move past it.... It's just may be tough right now whilst they are trying to get to the acceptance part.

I've learned to BE MY OWN BEST FRIEND. Look out for yourself. Stay away from negative, energy draining people. Stay away from people who don't want the best for you. You're not anti-them you're pro-you as my mom would say. Stick up for yourself, take your own advice. Give yourself constructive feedback. Just like you would for your best friend. Would you get them a little gift to let them know you're thinking of them? Get one for yourself too! Even if no one wanted to be my friend I like me, I'll just talk to myself all day until the doctors arrive with the white coats :)

I've learned that COMPASSION AND SELF-AWARNESS ARE VERY IMPORTANT. If you have these things you will be less offensive. Genuine compassion for others, to try to understand where they are, to try to be kind from the heart. Not a 'good Samaritan' that mugs people off because the motives are wrong. Acts of compassion that come from the heart are always rewarded. Awareness of yourself, how you are and how what you're doing and could be perceived helps to defuse difficult situations. Those who are not self-aware go through life wondering why no one likes them. Sometimes I've had to pull myself up on things. Was that really nice? Did I do that for the right reason? Am I coming across in a negative way?

I've learned that sometimes POSITIVITY IS ALL YOU HAVE! Sometimes you are down to nothing, and I mean nothing. No one can be there, you don't have anything. The only thing that can pull you through in that time is some good vibrations and a prayer. Even if nothing changes for a while if you keep going something will give. The law of attraction works, think about what you want and it will be drawn to you.

I've learned to DREAM BIG! When I decided I wanted to be on the TV in news I worked in Topshop in the changing rooms. What got me from one place to the other? Big dreams and single-minded vision. I just believed it would happen. It didn't happen with the job or the way I thought it would. But it happened. I'm still dreaming big and soon I'll have great news.

Having FAITH HELPS. I can't prove to someone who doesn't believe in God that he exists. But you can't prove he doesn't. I have found my faith a great help. Some say it's a crutch and yes it is. When times get hard you have to lean on something. To me it's comforting to believe that there is something bigger than all this.

I'm not a victim, I'm a survivor and in fact I'm an overcomer! Sometimes when the worst thing that can happen happens it's a chance to say the only way is up! It came along, I faced it, got knocked about a bit...BUT, I came back! It may take a while to get to the stronger bit, but just the fact you came back means you will get stronger.

I don't know why I wrote this today. I wasn't planning on sharing this like this. Sometimes losing a child is like a secret you can't tell anyone. People say oh when you get pregnant you'll understand and you want to say "I have been" but then you'll have to explain the whole story and so you don't. One of my personal aims and I'm not sure how, but it will happen, is to raise awareness of child-loss and to give a space for women who have lost babies at whatever time during their pregnancy a space to talk about it.

But for now, this morning I just want to say to anyone going through anything tough. No matter what comes you can keep going. Losing my daughter was so hard, I still cry sometimes. I cried last night, I still wish it didn't end like that. I thought I'd have another child by now, but it just hasn't gone that way. I could cry about it all the time and use it as an excuse to be sad and mope. BUT, something in me just doesn't allow it. As long as I have breath I have to keep going for the things I want. I believe I'll have children and get married and have the dream AND the career, yes I want it all. Why not, this is why I keep pushing. I'm not so strong, we all feel fear. But courage is what comes to help us push past the fear.

Someone once described it me like this: "Imagine yourself as a stained glass window. When something happens all the pieces are broken and on the floor. It's impossible to make the same picture again. Instead use the pieces to make a new beautiful picture."

Make new beautiful pictures everyone...x

You Can't Buy Time

What if you knew it was your last week, day or hour? What would you have done differently? Do it now.

Don't Let Anyone Steal Your Confidence

There's something about confident, assured and talented people that seems to really put certain other people on edge. But don't let anyone else's insecurity make you feel like you have to dim your light. We are ALL meant to shine!

You hear it quite often, "there's just 'something' about that person I don't like." If it can't be defined, it's probably nothing. Or, "who does he/she think is?" "Who do you think you're not?" Is the reply. Or the old chestnut of 'knocking the wind out of their sail (that'll show them)' reducing people, or helping them to 'know their place'.

I am confident and I have gone through a process to become it.

I'm not 'too big for my boots' I can assure you they fit just fine.

Don't let anyone steal your confidence. If you have completed your process and are on your path then just be you. Don't worry about your critics, they're not even in the game; they're on the side lines of life, just watching, sometimes wishing they could have a little of what you have. That is often the real issue.

What you think is normal, other people recognise as extraordinary.

SO, head up, shoulders back, face the world and inspire others by showing them what they can become if they find their confidence. Shine your light today.

"Our deepest fear is not that we are inadequate. Our deepest fear is that we are powerful beyond measure. It is our light, not our darkness that most frightens us. We ask ourselves, who am I to be brilliant, gorgeous, talented, and fabulous? Actually, who are you not to be?"

– Marianne Williamson

Great Expectations

How many times have you said, "I KNEW that was going to happen"? You literally attracted whatever 'that' was that you expected. So, start expecting great things to happen.

And Finally...

In news programmes, towards the end of the show, there is normally a story that we call the 'and finally' story

You've seen it. Singing cats, random old ladies who live in a shoe and other wacky stories!

These stories don't really fit anywhere else in the programme. They're not really news, but they are interesting or funny.

I love the movie 'The Holiday'. In it, Kate Winslet's character is told:

"You're acting like the best friend when you should be the leading lady!"

Sometimes we put ourselves second, third and last. We play second fiddle to family, friends and lovers, putting others before ourselves. There's nothing wrong with being selfless and kind. In fact, it's good for you!

Sometimes you can lose yourself trying to be everything to everyone else.

On an airplane they tell you if there's an emergency to put your oxygen mask on yourself first. Why? Because if you can't breathe, how can you help someone else?

You are your most valuable asset! Give to and love others, but remember to be the leading lady/man in your own life. Don't become the 'and finally' story in your own life, you need to be your top story!

The ones who really love you will understand that sometimes you need to put yourself first,

"If you don't like where you are MOVE! You are not a tree"

– Unknown

You Are The Master Of Your Fate

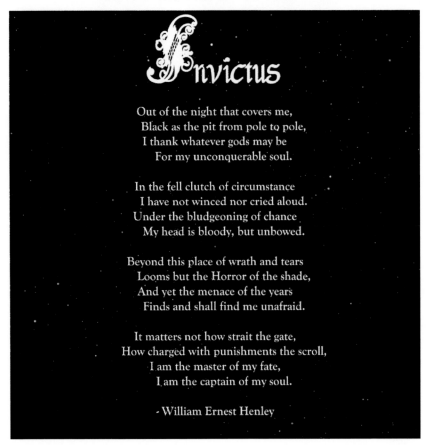

Invictus

Out of the night that covers me,
Black as the pit from pole to pole,
I thank whatever gods may be
For my unconquerable soul.

In the fell clutch of circumstance
I have not winced nor cried aloud.
Under the bludgeoning of chance
My head is bloody, but unbowed.

Beyond this place of wrath and tears
Looms but the Horror of the shade,
And yet the menace of the years
Finds and shall find me unafraid.

It matters not how strait the gate,
How charged with punishments the scroll,
I am the master of my fate,
I am the captain of my soul.

- William Ernest Henley

This poem gives me chills (the good kind). Whenever I think I can take no more. I read this! It makes me lift my head up. Don't react to everything that happens. Take charge, be the captain of your life.

Acknowledgments

Firstly thank you to our Father who art in Heaven. For the gifts of love, life and each new day.

For blessing me with an amazing family. My dad, Bishop Dr Joe Aldred, and my mom, Novelette Aldred. Thank you Mom and Dad for putting up with a diva middle child and always supporting me. My amazing sisters, Marsha and Alethea, who brought into the world my amazing nieces and nephews, Krystal, Arooj, Luke and Ellis; all of your love lifts me up, especially when I was very low. Alethea, thank you for your honesty in all things!

My wider family, especially Aunty Winsome (you have ALWAYS been there), Angie and my Grandma Pearline. Love you all like Jamaican food.

My fabulous friends who support me to the end. I will get in trouble as I will forget names! So those who encouraged me and gave me little nuggets for this book. Ronke Oke, Charmain Jackson, Leona Grant and Lauren Hampshire, as well as my sister Alethea, and parents who helped me bring this book to life.

There are three women I must thank. They advise me, pray for me, encourage me, and never let me give up! Julia Regis, Lee Joseph and Jennifer Wilson. Thank you from the bottom of my heart.

My heart is full of love for all my friends. Hopefully you know who you are! For those who stayed and those who left. I am grateful for you all.

To every person that has encouraged me, prayed for me, spoken well of me and lifted me up. Thank you.

Sade I know your purpose was fulfilled. When you left you gave me life. The love I had for you has forever changed me. You made me better than I was before you came and left. Rest in Peace.

About The Author

As a Journalist and TV Presenter Genelle has worked for the BBC, ITN, MailOnline and now ITV in various roles, including: online journalist, documentary producer, weather presenter and newsreader. Genelle has a Masters degree in Broadcast Journalism from Staffordshire University.

In addition to her media career, Genelle has her own business interests, she owns and runs an online boutique, SadeRose.

WEBSITE: www.genellealdred.com

FACEBOOK: www.facebook.com/genellealdredtv

TWITTER: @genellealdred